Poems From Underground

"'Deji Ayoade has penned a poignant poetry collection that not only pulls at one's heartstrings, but also invokes deep insight. Moreover, it inspires a sense of appreciation for life's inescapable troughs and crests through compelling verse."

-Eva Xan, Bestselling Poetry Editor & Author of Esoterra

Poems from Underground

A Memoir of Hope, Faith,
and the American Dream

by

'DEJI AYOADE

POEMS FROM UNDERGROUND

A Memoir of Hope, Faith, and the American
Dream By 'Deji Ayoade

Copyright © by 'Deji Ayoade

www.dejiayoade.com
ISBN: 979-8-9865876-4-6

For any information, please address 'Deji
Ayoade

at info@dejiayoade.com

or write to:

'Deji Ayoade

P.O. Box 4485

Broadlands, VA, 20148

Contents

PART 1:

Nigeria

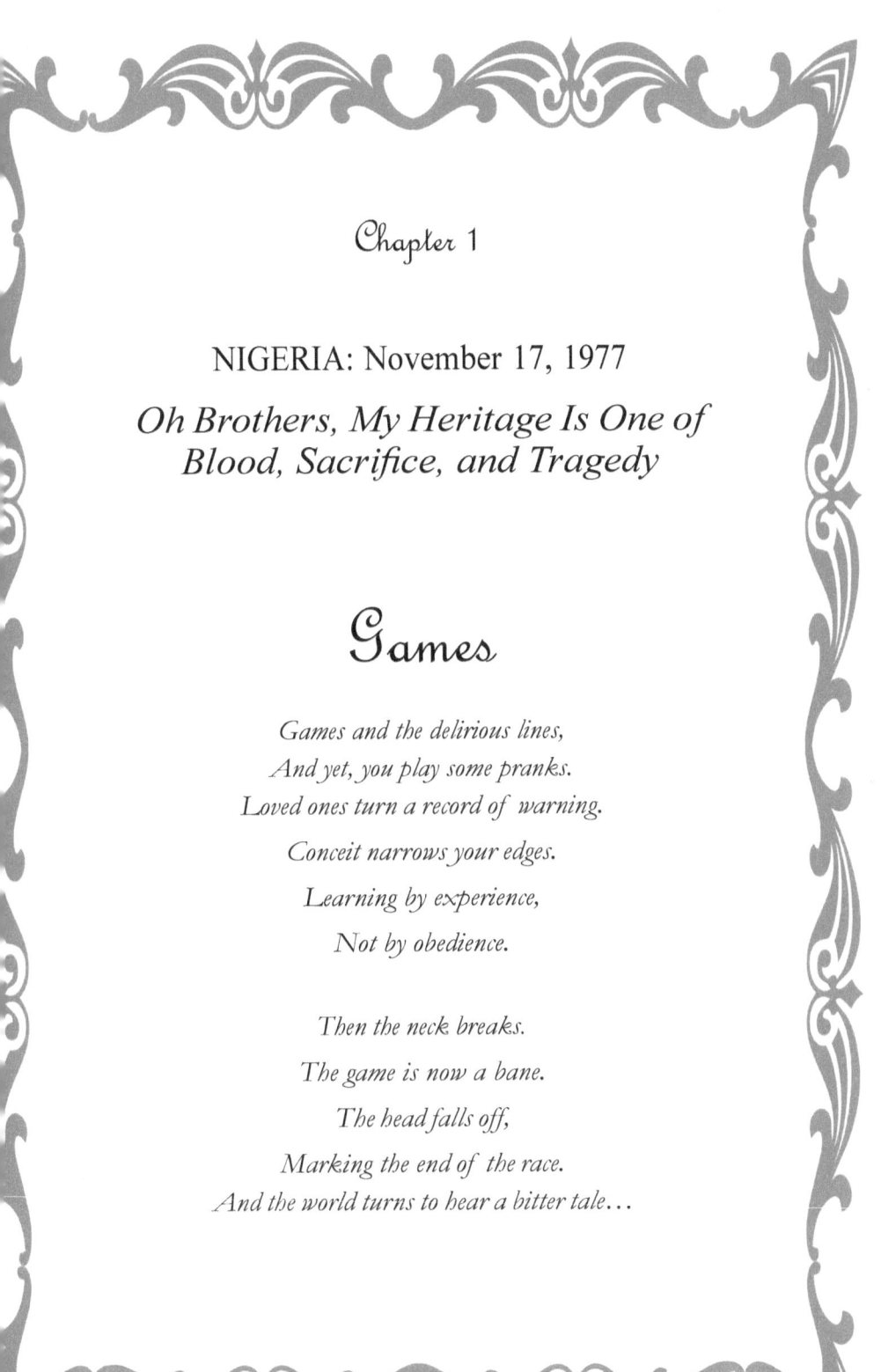

Chapter 1

NIGERIA: November 17, 1977

Oh Brothers, My Heritage Is One of
Blood, Sacrifice, and Tragedy

Games

Games and the delirious lines,
And yet, you play some pranks.
Loved ones turn a record of warning.

Conceit narrows your edges.

Learning by experience,

Not by obedience.

Then the neck breaks.

The game is now a bane.

The head falls off,

Marking the end of the race.
And the world turns to hear a bitter tale...

I'm a Runaway

As the clock ticked,
I wept in the solitary idleness of my mind,
Wishing I could take one more glance,
But I couldn't.
I wished I could wipe my tears,
But they fell on my heart.

With every step closer to my sanctuary,
Distance crawled in between.
I thought I found a new home,
But how could I survive a new Love?
Don't blame my fragile heart for growing in sorrow.
My hope was taken from me long ago.

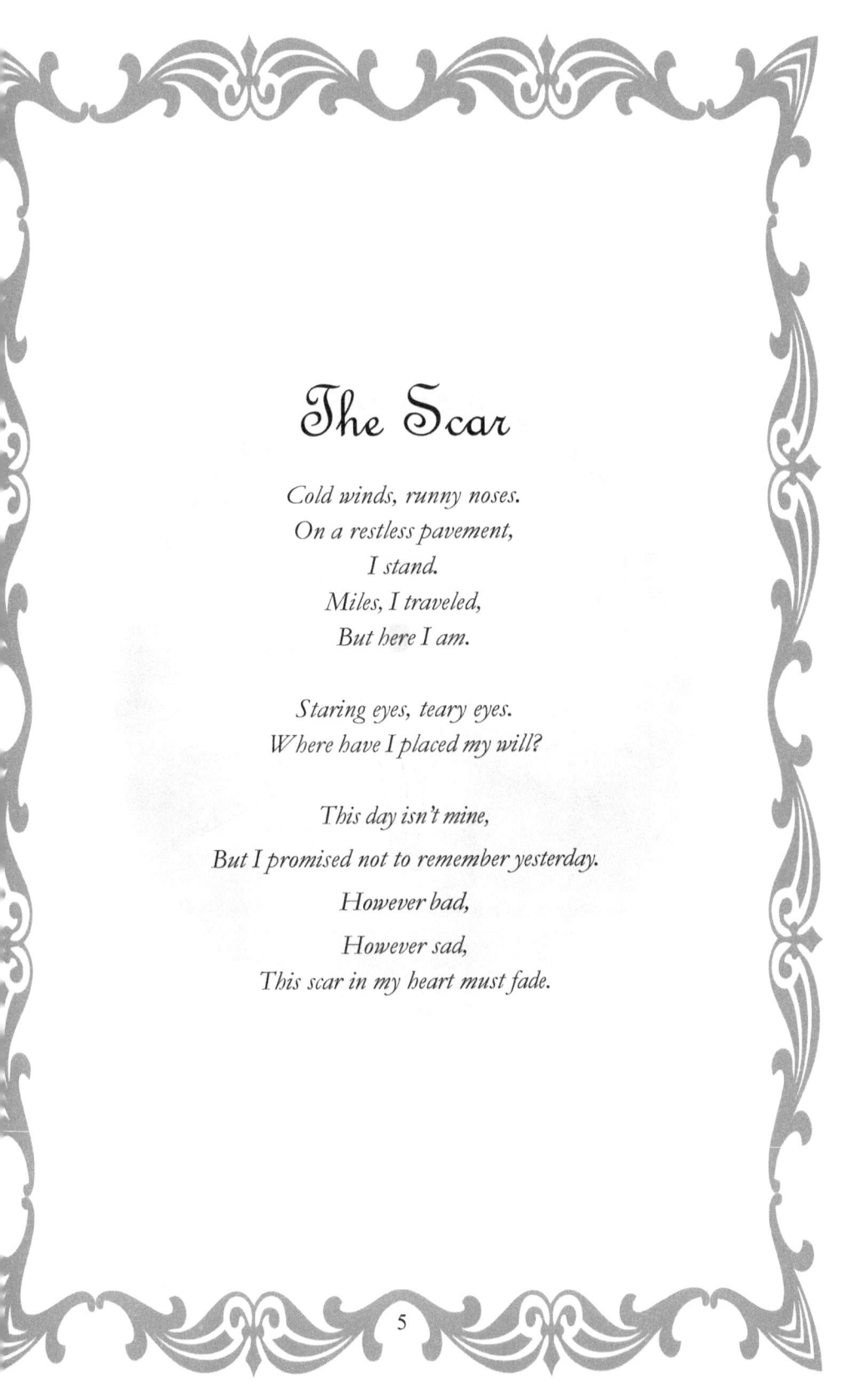

The Scar

Cold winds, runny noses.
On a restless pavement,
I stand.
Miles, I traveled,
But here I am.

Staring eyes, teary eyes.
Where have I placed my will?

This day isn't mine,
But I promised not to remember yesterday.
However bad,
However sad,
This scar in my heart must fade.

Chapter 2

NIGERIA: March 1987

The Housewarming

My Boat

I rock in my boat
As the waves glide beneath us.
The shimmering image of the sun
Sparkles upon my face in the gentle dusk.

Peace and joy are my friends.
We paddle with ease and care.
The sea smiles at me, and the blue sky's
Reflection is her beautification.
I smile back,
And we salute each other.

I'm tossed in my boat!
I cannot see him,
But how he deals with me...
Dark cumulus o'er my head gather.
Bright swords are blinding my way.

Driven by reckless tornadoes,
Black waters slap against my boat.

Marked and dampened,
A rugged flare—my face.
I am alone—who watches me?
I am torn—who mocks me?
But she stands firm, my feet held—Love.

When my beloved boat broke,
After high seas and low,
Currents, canals, and caverns
Around the small globe,
I rested with her.
Then I landed on the mighty's land,
Before the king whose eyes are keen,
For scales appeared in it.
How did you keep her?

Forlorn. Here I am now.

Your Time

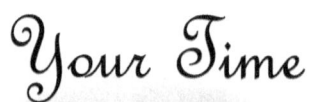

Hurt you, hurt me,
We both must feel.
Hate pain, love pain,
She will always have a place.
How long, how well,
You must be stronger at the
end.

Don't get me wrong
'Cause my pain won't last long.
Sorrow won't last forever,
But I can choose which memories
will linger.

Finally, the lessons
Will open your eyes to your blessings.
It's all for a purpose,
That which fate proposed.
You may never realize
Until the right time—
Your time.

Chapter 3

NIGERIA: July 1990

A Needle to the Heart

It's Alright

I have been with you,
And you said, "Certainly, I do know."
The sea tide is rising,
So let's go home.
Home is in the end—
The end of a long road.
It haunts me to tell,
That this, you must tread.

It's so uncertain—
I'm sorry,' urn request.
The thorns must be there,
Including the starless midnights,
And as in the beginning,
You don't have to find me.
No! You'll never walk alone.
Everything is alright.

These bloody drains—
Is it that of domestics?
She looked at me and sighed.
"It may be cruel as you see it.
Perhaps as you take it or live it
It has little purpose—
To bother or worry.
There will always be tomorrow,
So please don't hurry."

My son... my help!
Well, it's just me now.
The road, this road we're on.
No cars, no flight; so dull.
I won't be afraid of surprises.
I'm full of it.

"Looking back is bad.
There's no need to look around,"
She whispered from afar.
"Well, then, help me to not look down.
And if I look inside,
Tell me it will be alright."
"Hey, son!" she whispered aloud,
"But these rights include so many ways of life:
The thins, crooks, and smooth.
Teach me to look up."
Then she said, "That's all right."

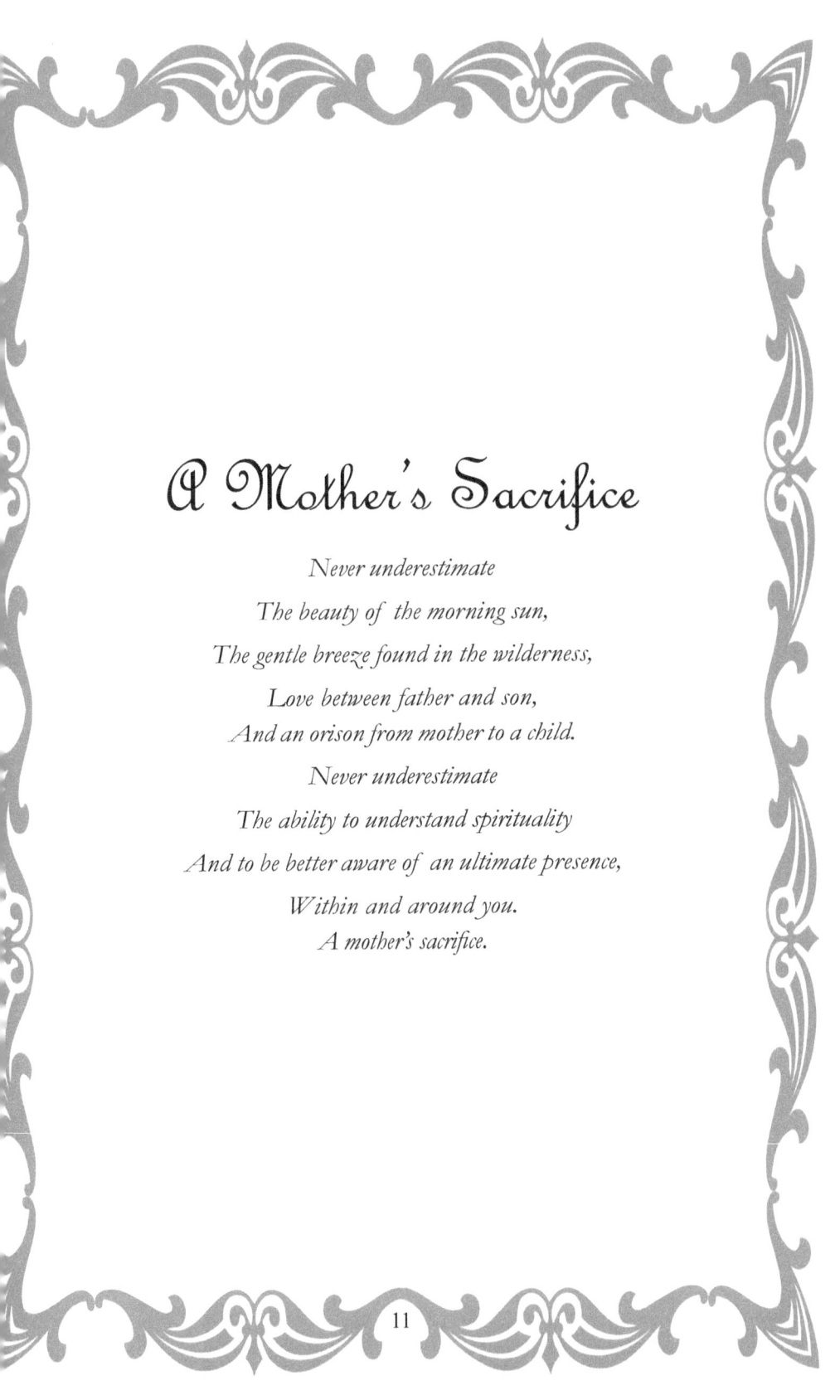

A Mother's Sacrifice

Never underestimate
The beauty of the morning sun,
The gentle breeze found in the wilderness,
Love between father and son,
And an orison from mother to a child.
Never underestimate
The ability to understand spirituality
And to be better aware of an ultimate presence,
Within and around you.
A mother's sacrifice.

Blue Rose in the Star

I was only four
When she told me they were stars.
Up in the night sky,
They never stopped shining.

That's where I wanted to be,
But there was no one to take me there.
For years, I watched so intently,
But I could only see my reflection
Down at my feet.

I'm twenty-eight,
And I still haven't stopped.
I have the picture of a blue rose in my star,
And it makes me think of who you are.
I see a shadow of a woman watching me,
And it reminds me of what your Love is.

So many times, I've thought about my life,
And how much pain it's caused yours.
I could live without everything else,
But not without your Love, mama.

Chapter 4

NIGERIA: 1990

No One but Alhaja

You are my haven.
I could burrow up and down
In the letters of your words
And find clarity in your wisdom.

Your Love is my refuge.
I could reminisce
About all that was more than words
And burn in memories of you.

Between joy and sorrow is time and knowledge,
And I could still pour my heart out
Just to find
How to live right by you—my solace.

Staying Alone

Staying alone is a task to deal with.
Staying alone—O, for a man to be
Like red coal sinking into the still sea…
Staying alone amid turmoil.
Staying alone, yet amidst many.

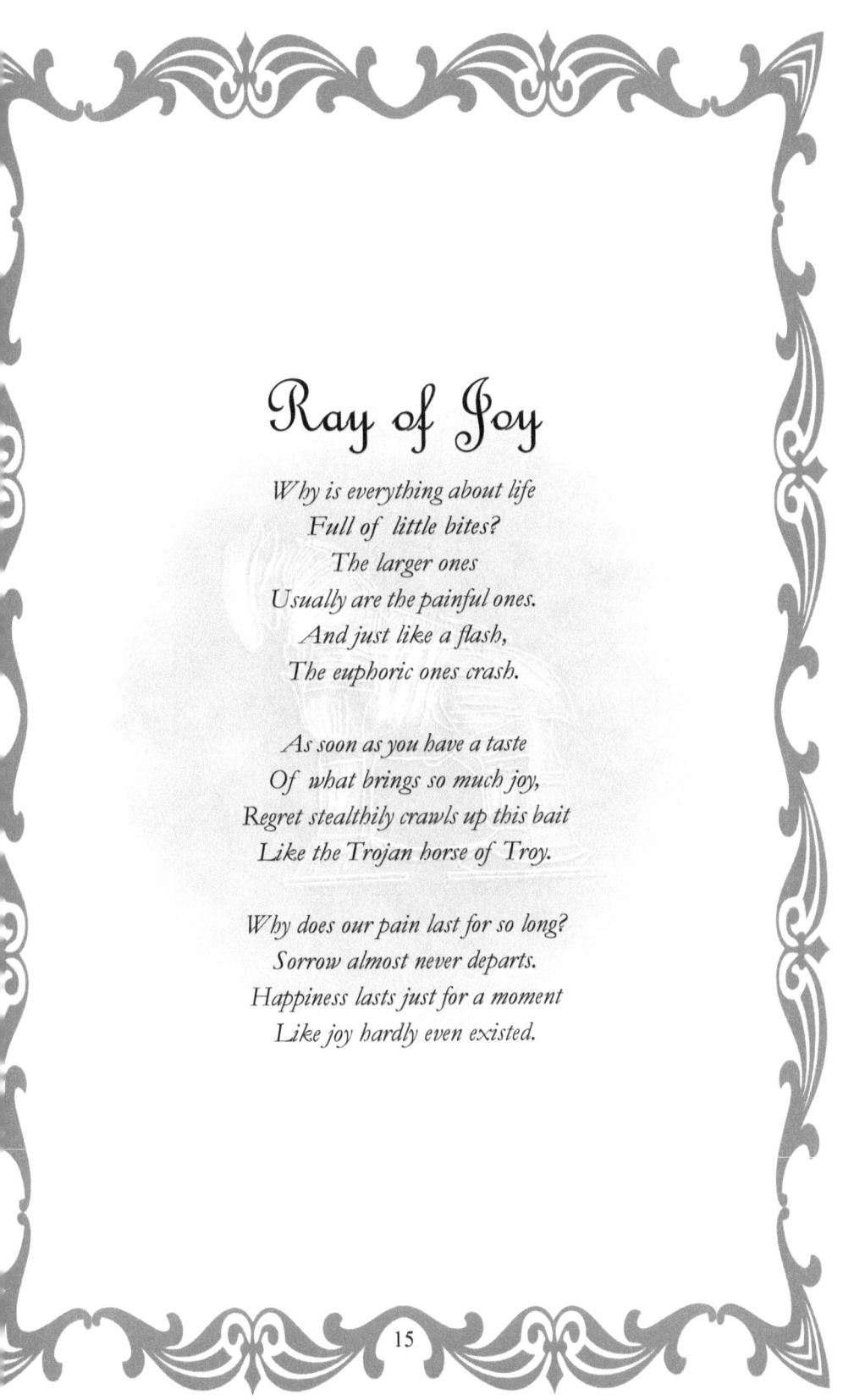

Ray of Joy

Why is everything about life
Full of little bites?
The larger ones
Usually are the painful ones.
And just like a flash,
The euphoric ones crash.

As soon as you have a taste
Of what brings so much joy,
Regret stealthily crawls up this bait
Like the Trojan horse of Troy.

Why does our pain last for so long?
Sorrow almost never departs.
Happiness lasts just for a moment
Like joy hardly even existed.

Chapter 5

NIGERIA: 1995

Idolatry with Cozener

Free Thinker

One love, one heart, one life,
Everyone.
Humanity and its reproach.
The dint in that eye.
That look that besmirches.
She can never be yours.
Not for the times,
Not for the procedures,
But for a faith that stands firm.

What we made makes us—
What we believe separates us.
The blood and the water,
The numerous sacrifices
In the name of Christ,
Or perhaps a God that can't fight.
The enmity of humanity sits
With ethnicity and self-belief.

The freedom we cry about
Is not in the loosened
Shackles of independence.
Independence lies in
The freedom of our minds.
It's better to be a free-thinker
Than a heavenly murderer.

It's better to be originless
Than to be a kinsman killer.
I would live in all the darkness
Rather than hate in lightness.

I won't serve a God who has
No better way to the truth,
Nor will I be a brother to
Those ethnocentric fools.
I would be an island
And live free, serve free, love free!

Chapter 6

NIGERIA: 1997

Moonlight over the Balcony

Why?

Down my arms,
Roll the tears
From the corners of my eyes.

On the radio
Is a young rodeo
From a sad little town.

In the rhythm of the music,
I feel an empty life hanging on to a wish.
My soul's heavy
And my eyes are teary.

There have been
So many disappointments,
And I dread this could be the life meant for me.
I wish I had all the answers to my questions,
But all I can do is pray for a vision.

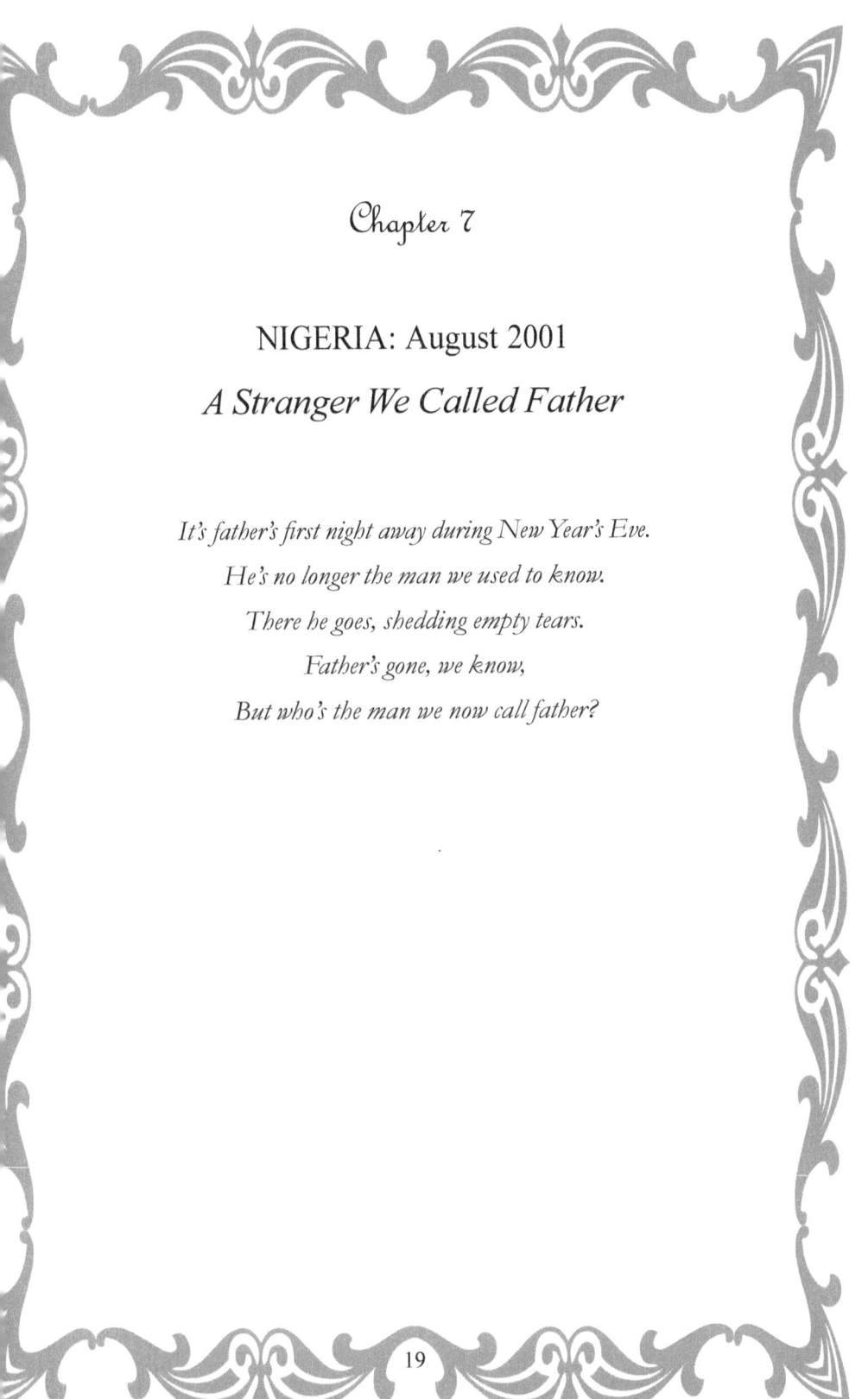

Chapter 7

NIGERIA: August 2001
A Stranger We Called Father

It's father's first night away during New Year's Eve.
He's no longer the man we used to know.
There he goes, shedding empty tears.
Father's gone, we know,
But who's the man we now call father?

Shako

In a manic phase,
Five young busters race.
Every element is possessed.
Too small was the closet,
Yet you're locked all the way in.

Shako, the brave one!
A man of heart and Love.
Mighty in frame, fearsome in stature.
To his fears, he never turned his back,
And to the weak, he sacrificed his life.

Shako, I see tears in your heart;
You're about to end your own life.
You're in there,
But your world couldn't see you.
You will walk through that door,
But you will never make it back.
And the rest of us
Can only mourn you
For the rest of our lives.

Instincts

Some people walk
And others run,
But I move like a rolling stone.
It never stops;
It's the reason I never give up.

Some people keep their eyes open
Or leave them closed.
Others prefer their eyes wide shut,
But mine are like that of an eagle;
I see what others don't see.

Some people cry
And others weep.
Tears can only be wiped off the face
But can never be stopped from shedding.
I still give thanks for my sorrow.

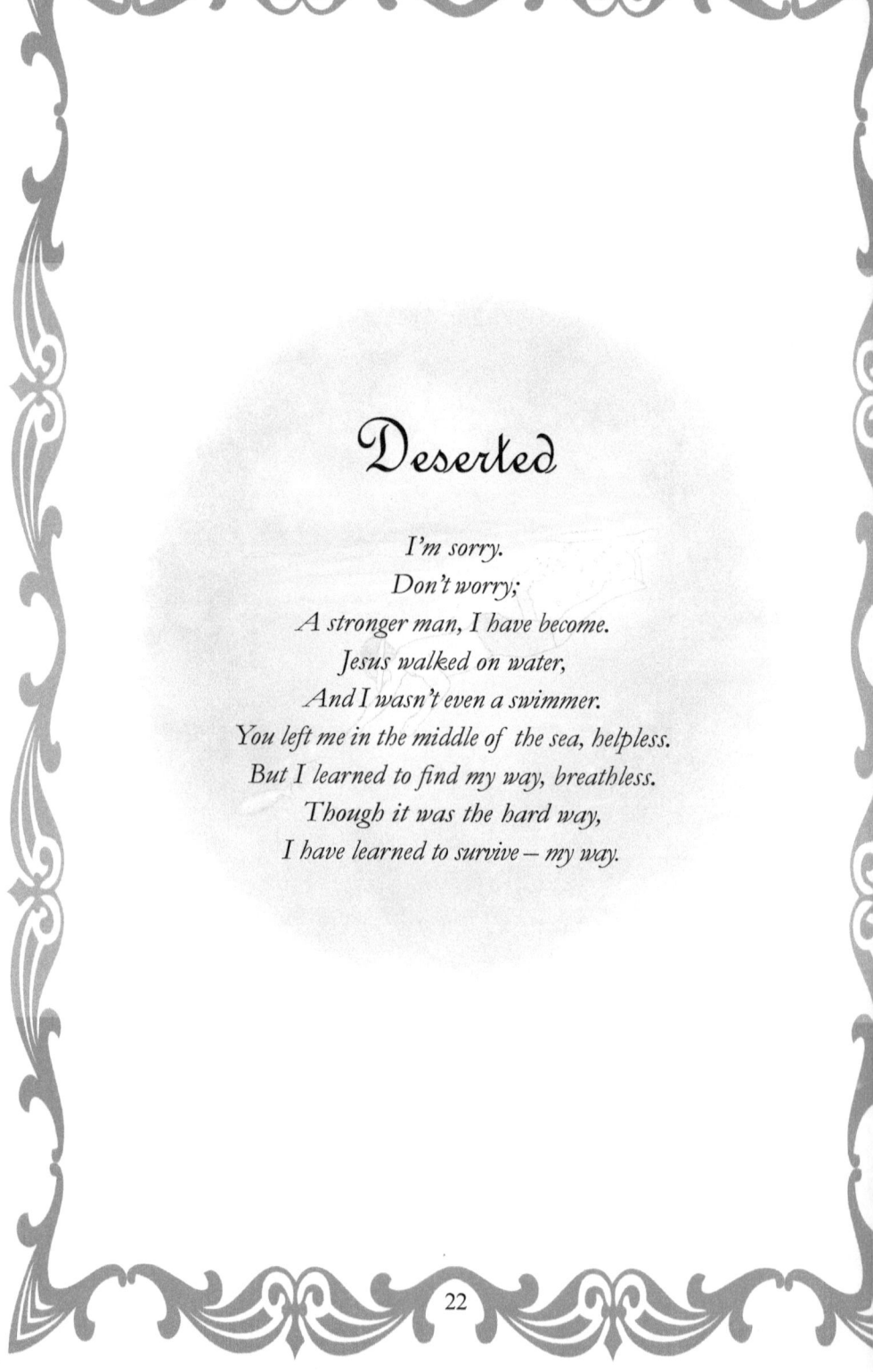

Deserted

I'm sorry.
Don't worry;
A stronger man, I have become.
Jesus walked on water,
And I wasn't even a swimmer.
You left me in the middle of the sea, helpless.
But I learned to find my way, breathless.
Though it was the hard way,
I have learned to survive — my way.

Chapter 8

NIGERIA: November 2006

Dead Man's Purgatory

Elevator to Heaven

So meek, life's journey can be,
And what couldn't be averred
Makes it contrastive.

I once took off like an eagle,
Soared so high,
And held everything beneath
In the palm of my hand.
I touched the sky,
And no soul could comprehend how.
I stood in the sun,
But didn't get burned.
I wined and dined on the moon
And shared a crown.

Still, nothing's changed.
The pieces of every path seemingly lost
Only lead to the break of a new dawn.

How much more time will I squander
While plying the road to my dream?
How many mountains, oceans, and seas will I cross?
I need to understand the voice
That was echoing so loud
I could barely unravel its words,
Though I knew where it was coming from...

The Wait

Have you ever felt like you live in
A different world in your mind?
You can smell it, see it, and feel it...
Every moment of your breath!
A million fragments of varying visions,
You can't quite explain it.
Even so, the urge is undeniable:
Never stop running!
It is your future without a doubt!

You keep chasing after yourself.
It looks as though it's thousands
Of years away from you.
The closer you get,
The more it feels like
You have taken a wrong turn
At one imperceptible point.
Alas, you're at a halt,
Pondering and seeking,
Where next to turn,
Peradventure, the time you could procure,
Or so you reckon.

As it seems toilsome to align
The pieces of your own puzzle,
You perceive for certain that time waits—
Time which has been indomitable.

Call it impatience;
I call it one life to fulfill—
A life I can't help but helplessly and patiently wait for,
Even when it's the most grueling thing to do.

Chapter 9

NIGERIA: November 2007

A Cat with Nine Lives

A Bruise in My Heart

Why would your vision be the same
When I keep you out of my sight?
Why would your memories remain
If I keep you out of my mind?
Why do stones thrown in anger
Only hurt twice as much?

Staring at the sender
Only makes me feel worse.
I am empty inside,
So like a dead leaf, endlessly, I float.
No one could ask why,
'Cause I found myself in a blank world alone.

I wish that beating
heart,
In the world I so crave,
Could hear my plight,

As I drifted, waiting to be saved.
They say that hearts won't stay broken,
And I'm afraid
The bruise in my still heart will never heal.

Mirage

I have no alternate lives;
There is just this one season,
A generation of existence.
It's one in which I spend my time
In an absolute fritter.
I have a colossal mind
But cannot bring it to life.

There's only one reason—
As if my hands are bound
By a mortal sin, and I attest that I'm fine.
And how—why—am I always three?
There are so many thoughts
And nothing's done,
Like twinkling stars fading in and out.
Ideas, like a river, flow,
With nowhere to call home.

The agonies of living lie in the regret of the past.
Oh, that I may hang these shirts and buy a new one,
And how it haunts me so to realize
You've been squandering your time.
Everything is by grace,
Not by power or might,
And my productivity is only a proclivity,
Not veracity.

I deserve no pardon but clemency.
It's getting bad… verily, he works hard.

I wish I could work now, that it would work out
And burn all these shirts up!
The man of this morning is another—
Another tomorrow evening, even this night.
How my life is like a mirage!

There are so many worries
Of the past and the future times,
But how to make today materialize is unrealized.
So, what do I do now?
With these sour comments and whining,
Heaven, wake me from these
Nightmares and make me what I ought to be.

I count on your chance
So much—I need to be found
By you so enrich me.
I just hope, in you, somehow—anyhow—
And above all, my faith, I believe in you.

Chapter 10

NIGERIA: February 2008

One Last Hug from Father

Sleep

Did you know, son,
That living fires get scared?
They grow legs
And make haste while being chased.
Oh, son, by circumstance's pranks.
Who knows his stand?
Who knows his fate?
Strong bows break
When bent by strong hands.
So now you see why we have to fear...

Fear? Why fear?
Fear the fall of mighty men.
Fear the fall of righteous men.
Fear the fall of able men.
All ridiculed, most miserable—
Their stead.

Son, that's the end:
When the weak oppose the strong
And the dogs beat the lions—
When material withstands ethereal,
And darkness breaks boundaries with light.

The fetters never loose.
Spider webs are good
Enough to entwine.
Long you'll tarry in blue.
You'll think you're two.
The race—this race is but doom.
Delicate world,
Weak hearts.
Fragile souls wait to be swallowed.
There's confusion all day long,
But grace is so strong.

So, humbly be bold,
And let those shoulders hold.
For we don't know who goes
By treating life like clothes
'Cause truly, it wears out, becoming old.
Men are waiting vipers,
Venom spat about.
But, watch—don't sleep.
Watch on this steep.

The Point of No Return

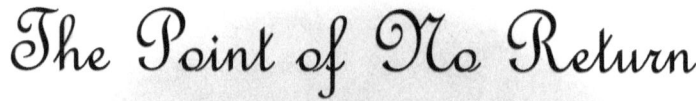

All your life,
You wished for the painless rest.
Time showed no mercy,
For you squandered all chances.

Tomorrow,
You wished to make things right.
Your days came shorter than you planned,
For your fate wasn't entirely in your hands.

Once a lion,
The world could hear you.
You wished to roar one more time.
With your days numbered,
All hope was gone...

Smile

Smile—
The many hours of life are but rose flowers;
Every single day is a blossom that withers.
But it's hard to understand the certainty of death,
Even though his cold hands are ever-present.
Life is short but looks long.
Life is too short to sluggishly live on.

Yes, smile—
For every rising sun begins in God's might.
And do not remember your sorrows,
But borrow those experiences for tomorrow.
Register the lessons of the mistakes,
And then open every letter in hope, not fear.

Please, smile—
'Cause if we consider the past,
The bitterness, and offenses,
We will never live for a better task,
As the sun will never set on our profound sense.
The best thing to do, my dear, is to forge ahead.

Now, smile—
There's nothing as easy to carry as a light heart,
For troubles and problems are a part of every life,
And what makes a man is his courage in spite
To pick every good part and emerge standing.
So, come on, smile—it's never ever hard.

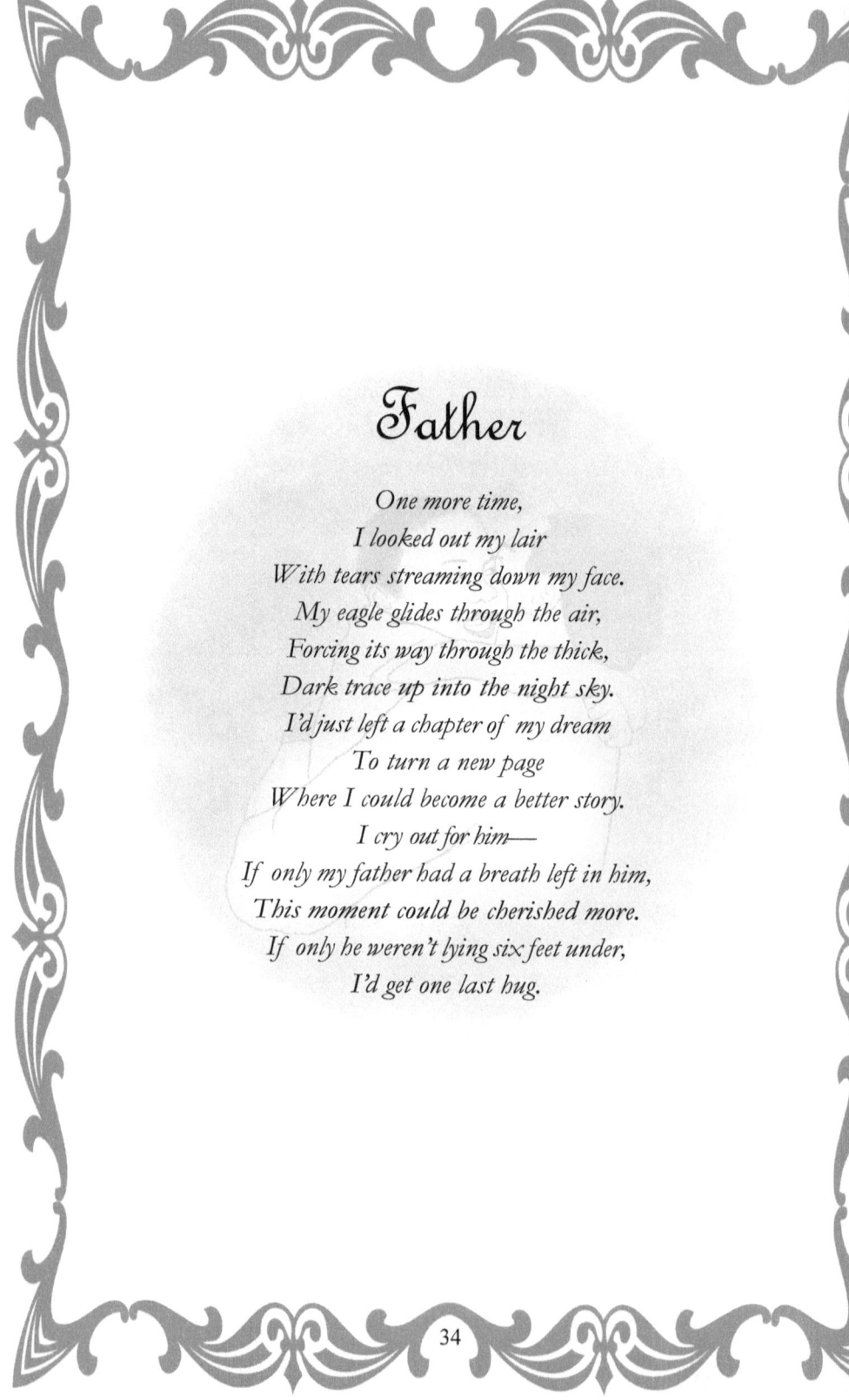

Father

One more time,
I looked out my lair
With tears streaming down my face.
My eagle glides through the air,
Forcing its way through the thick,
Dark trace up into the night sky.
I'd just left a chapter of my dream
To turn a new page
Where I could become a better story.
I cry out for him—
If only my father had a breath left in him,
This moment could be cherished more.
If only he weren't lying six feet under,
I'd get one last hug.

PART 2:

America

Chapter 11

BALTIMORE, MD: November 2008

A Missing Piece

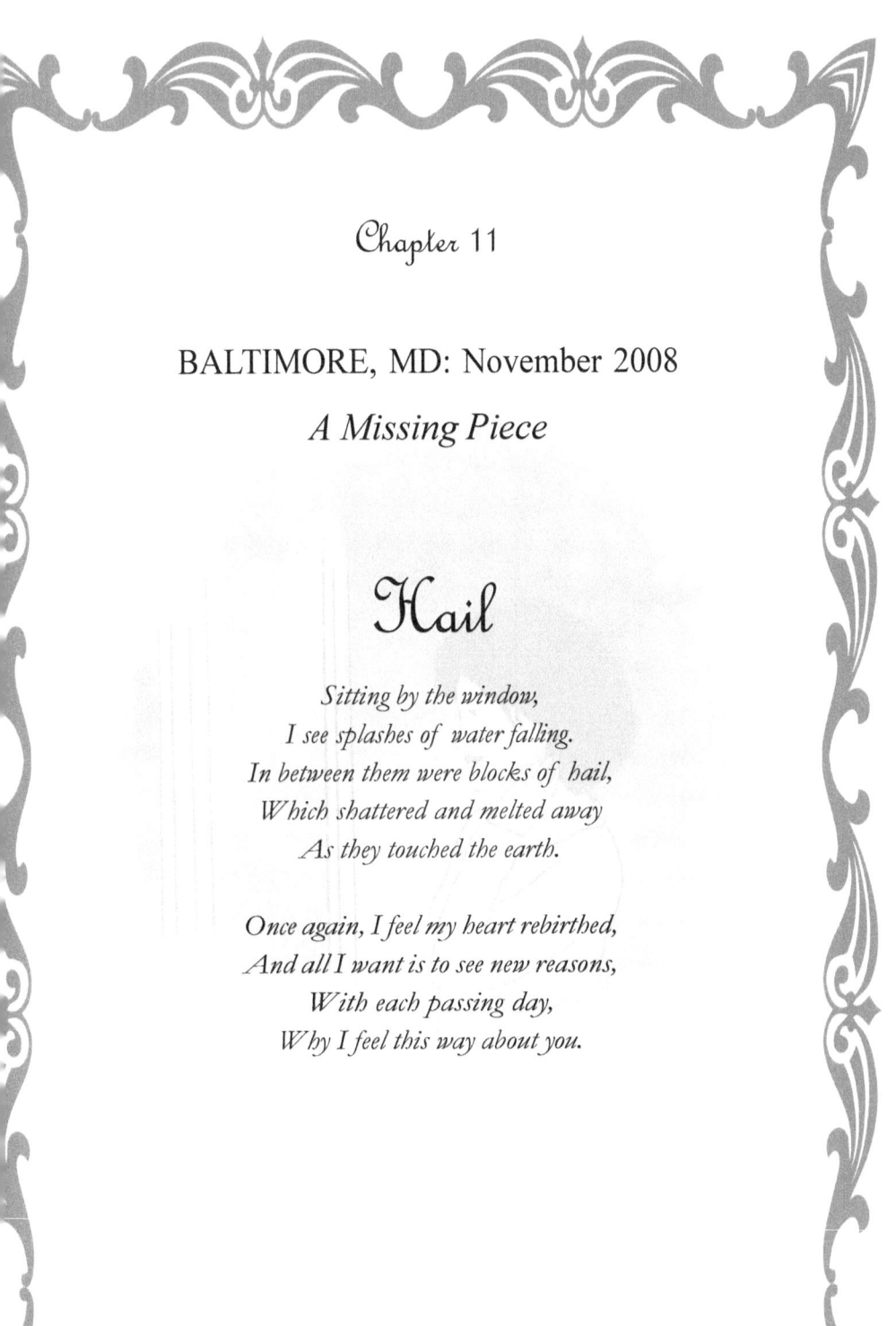

Hail

Sitting by the window,
I see splashes of water falling.
In between them were blocks of hail,
Which shattered and melted away
As they touched the earth.

Once again, I feel my heart rebirthed,
And all I want is to see new reasons,
With each passing day,
Why I feel this way about you.

Forever

I *love you!*
O, to say this a thousand times.
I would gladly place upon me
A duty
To sit and exclaim,
"I love you always!"

If not for the sun's uncompromising stand
And the moon's inconsistency,
I would journey across the universe with you.
If not for the cold winds of the dark heavens' time
And the brightness of the yellow star,
We would dine in the night sky
Fifty times to discuss your hair.

If not for nature's call,
The catalog of daily chores,
The ancient curse of man to toil—
Including your impatience—
I would sacrifice all my time
Seventy times to admire your lovely eyes.

If not for the old folks' eyes
And the altar call on Sundays
Making the conscience lush and red,
I would be a slave to my desires
A hundred times to make you wild.

And if not for the certain silence,
The serene underground,
Or the time to sail to Hades's end,
Where all passions are lost to time,
I would journey to the edge of the seas.
For eternity, I'm yours, mademoiselle.

Chapter 12

NEW YORK CITY, NY: 2009

A Friend

Only You

I recall the first time I set eyes on you,
I heard the sound of my laughter.
For a moment,
My heart did not believe it,
But my mind reminded me otherwise,
As I tried to make sense of it.

Lonely times passed by…
Though they weren't troubled times,
Especially with a radio nearby,
Playing such a beautiful song.
Several wishes,
With wonderful imaginations
Filled my thoughts.

How I wish to be by your side always.
Howbeit, you will always be with me,

In my thoughts,
In my imagination,
In my joy,
In my sorrow,
In my heart,
And in every breath.
Just you, only you.

Who Is Your Friend?

Darkness, light; denial clarity!
That's what happens
When you finally understand life isn't entirely
What you believed it not to be.
Wildebeests will always flock together, so would Zebras,
Pondering about it is a complete waste of time.
There isn't much you can do about it...

The Art of Love

If man could understand
That Love is the greatest gift,
If he would always take a stance
For virtuousness to win,
Then he would fathom Love.

If Love is more than just a feeling
Straight from the heart,
And if we write and sing about Love
As if it is a craft,
Then trust me, Love is beauteous.

If physical intimacy alone doesn't account for
Love, and you oppose vanity for Love,
If your Love is pure,
Then what more?
Your Love is true.

Midnight Princess

In the beating rhythm of the African drum,
She made a cast as an artist draws,
Her light brown skin, a tanned bronze.

Spinning like a drunken one,
With an enchanting demonic phrase,
She creates vivid mind-spells.

We were enthralled by the moonlight dance
Of the dour, cold mademoiselle,
Whose twist of torso spreads
A detailed innuendo sense.

The face, replicate of Aphrodite,
With an aura of femme fatale.
Our canonical tale,
Now of abstract menace.

As eyes sparkled like the starry night,
The waist whirled, wheeled an 'S',
And the waist created a gentle air caress.

Like a legion's possession,
She delicately stretched
And laid a pattern on the dark earth.
Indifferent to the Sahara gale,
She burned like a naked goddess.

As she controlled the wind and air,
For all to respect and stare
Like a midnight flame, she burned red.
Hooding our mind in mocking play,
Hail, princess of the dark day!

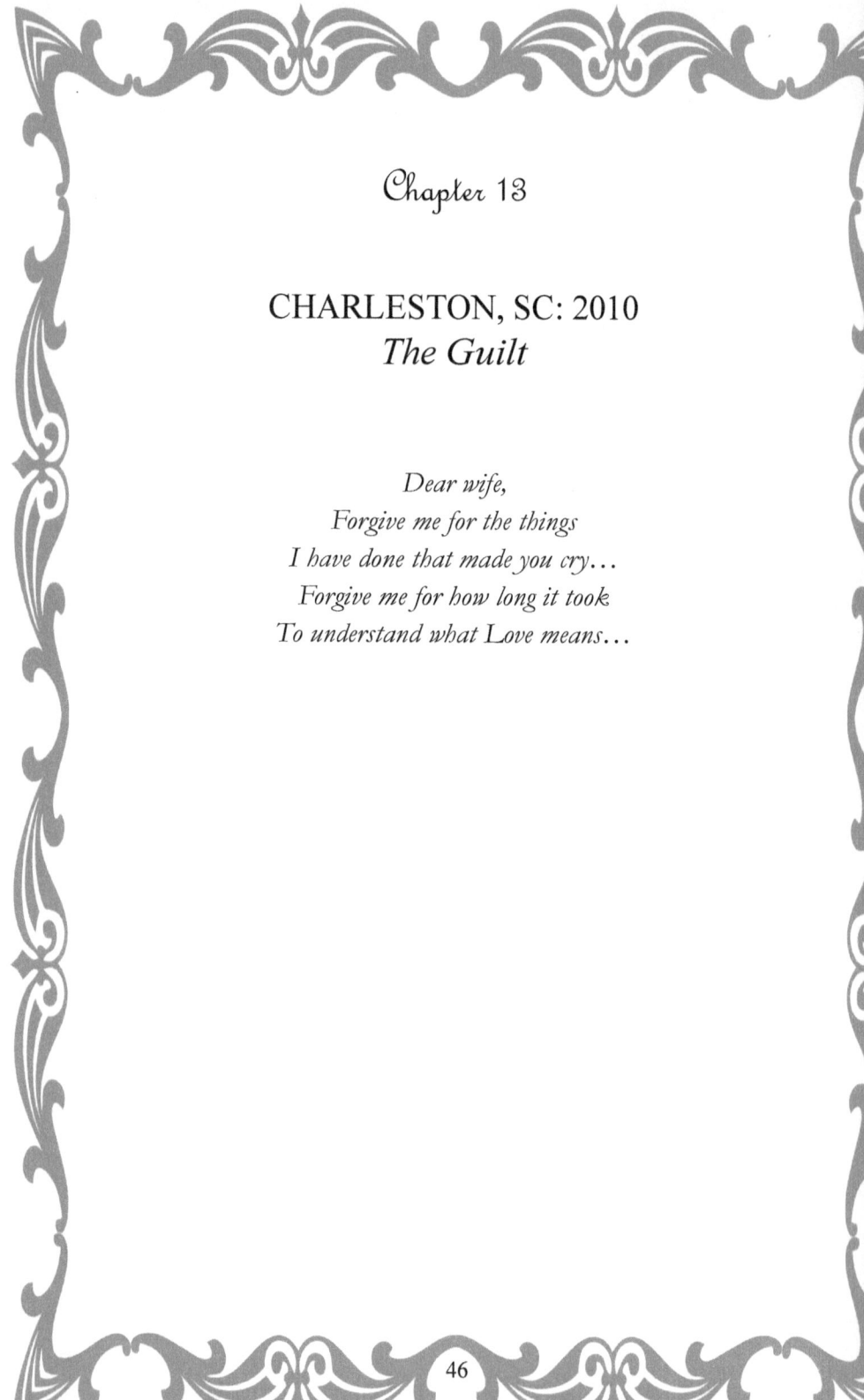

Chapter 13

CHARLESTON, SC: 2010
The Guilt

Dear wife,
Forgive me for the things
I have done that made you cry…
Forgive me for how long it took
To understand what Love means…

Forgive Me

I always thought I knew the man in the mirror,
And that's why I still saw a sheep,
Even when I turned into a wolf.

But you have,
And that's why you chose me.
How was I to know
I could turn on one of mine someday?

Beneath my innocence
Thrive my greatest fears.
Like the easy drag of the water by the riverbank,
I never comprehend how much danger.

My callousness haunts me,
And like heroin gushing through veins,
My greatest desire is to have your forgiveness.

Believe

I should have taken a trip into
your world,
Then I probably could understand
you more.
You have built for yourself a
castle of fear
So weak, a gentle breeze it
couldn't bear.

I caused you so much pain,
But we can start all over again.
If every pain that I put you
through
Remains alive in you,
Then every trial,
Would be mine.

I have empty shoulders to lean
on—
Would you let me be the one?
I have listened to so many songs,
And I have waited for so long,
But I choose to believe in this
Love,
And in it, I want to live
Forevermore.

Tonight

Tonight,
I wonder where you are
And what you are doing.

Are you crying just as I am,
Or lying in someone else's arms?
Is your bed dampening with tears,
Or are you laughing happily with someone else?

What I feel is more than pain.
How long will things be this way?
Although it took so much time to realize,
You have always been right.

Heaven on Earth
Never comes by trying too hard;
Only a confused heart does.
It is not only about being loved,
But loving,
Living a life not only mine,
But ours—
Not just my dream,
But ours.

Don't turn us into a beaut
Without tomorrow.
Hail from heaven,
Without a place to fall,
For your Love is peace to my heart.
Love is you and me forever.

Words of Wisdom

Never marry for Love,
Marry for friendship.
Never sleep a night,
Heart heavy with malice;
It's a complete waste of emotion.

Never make Love
Just because you can,
Make love for the bond it brings.

You can count the friends you've missed,
But reminisce more on the good times you've shared—
Somehow, you will always find them
In this life or the next.

Dwelling in your past
Is like holding on to a map
That only sets you back on your path
But can't guide you toward your future.

If you're to hold on to your past,
Let it guide your future.
Unavoidable situations are unfortunate,
So we believe.
To have perfect control of one's future
Can be more destructive.
Fate is an element to believe in
And a good excuse not to have ambition.

I hate to admit it,
But it's true:
No man would triumph,
Without the sacrifice of another.
The philosophy of good only comes from bad,
Success from failure,
And a cathedral from crumbs of destruction.

Knowledge

I've learned never to lie to the woman of my dreams.
What really matters is that you're real,
And not what you want to be—
Life might deny you a deal.

I've learned to listen to my heart-call
And not my head-toll—
To seize the world
Before it seizes me.
Beware of fate!

I've learned to make choices that fulfill dreams.
You may never comprehend faith,
But you know your dreams.
Your dreams may be your fate,
So why let go?

I've learned not to be a dreamer
Who makes a good lover when it's darker
But cannot be depended on
As soon as the morning comes.

Ma Reine

If how much time we spent with someone
Was a measure of our thoughts about them,
Then twenty-four hours a day
Would be as trivial as the star I can't see
Every night up in the sky,
As to the wishes of my heart.

If I had thought of those years to come
With holidays, woods, snow, children,
Grandchildren, and gray hairs,
And in between those years,
We would share moments of laughter and tears,
Then my life couldn't be without you.

If I dreamt of memories with you,
Walking side by side, hand in hand, eyes to eyes,
And never part,
Then that moment is now.

Moments I would call right back
After an argument to tell you I adore you;
Moments you would cry on my shoulder
And smile back at my humor;
Moments I would watch you fall asleep on my chest
And feel the warmth of your breath on my neck.

Queen, tu es la belle vie que je cherche.
If Love is the greatest

Gift to share and treasure,
It lives within you.

If Love is faith
That dream will come true,
Then you are real.

And if Love is so beautiful
It can't be described,
Then amour tu es.

PART 3:

U.S. Navy & U.S. Air Force

Chapter 14

NEW YORK CITY, NY: April 2011
Anchors Aweigh

Gaze

The warmest day of my life,
I stood by your side
And held you in my hands.
When you looked into my eyes,
I couldn't help but wish to tell you
How much I wanted to share my dreams with you.

Times change,
The truth unfurls.
I never felt in so much of a hurry,
For there was so much to bury.

Many promises have been kept in my heart,
And so little hope has been left alive,
But I know for sure,
In you, my dreams will survive.

Profound

Tonight,
In the solitary ray of my thoughts,
Resounding in my head
As I recall his words,
I remembered the past
And the promises I made at his cast.

I finally have a reason,
The flaming desire to succeed.
Every promise made,
Needed not—I have traced
That the future never stops,
And in my dreams, I am tossed.

I will get there,
Not someday,
But till I die,
I will always get there!

Chapter 15

SAN DIEGO, CA: September 2011
What Will Be, Will Be

I've come to realize
That hastening can be childlike.
Patience has become a rare virtue.
Excellence is the purest beauty.

I've come to realize that
The beginning of a man's future
Starts from the moment
He understands the need to be part of the world
And strives to make the best out of it.

I've come to realize that
In my destiny,
Lies my fate and the earth's hereafter.
And in my journey
Across the deserts and the seas,
I overcame the tides, storms, and whirlwinds
'Cause my faith could move the massif.

I've come to realize that,
Not only could destiny be discerned,
It could also be a bright and beautiful reflection
Of your muse and dreams.

The words you say and what you believe,
Each step you take, and the path you tread
Will make who you become.
Even though it may not be
On the near side of your knowing,
Your faith can see you through if you let it.

Chapter 16

SAN DIEGO, CA: November 2013
A Dying Tree at My Door

Numb

I lie awake on a Saturday morning,
Completely numb.
I can't tell how far I've gone this time.
I feel like a bag of sorrow,
Seeking a heart to spill.
I feel like a bunch of floating cloud,
Tied up,
And I can't tell if heaven is listening anymore.

Something is eating me up,
Bit by bit;
I can only feel the pain in my heart,
But I can't tell where it's coming from.
The desire to break away
Aches badly in my soul.

A voice says, "Suicide's a perfect way out,"
But I don't even want to think of a way out,
'Cause I'm scared that if I leave,
I might end up someplace worse.

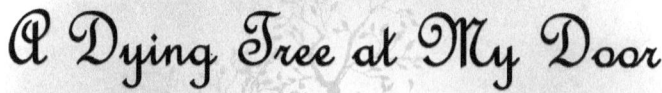

A Dying Tree at My Door

"Save me! Save me!"
A dying tree at my door
Cried out to me.
"My leaves are falling,
And the wind is coming.
Save me! Save me!
Lest I die…"

The Nightmare

Brown leaves, brown leaves,
They drop on my field.
Sorrow, pain; sorrow, pain,
Like a gravid sparrow, nests in my brain.
Fragile heart, fragile heart,
Tell me, will I die?
My soul, my house,
What's become of my life?

King Jotham

O', King Jotham!
Remember me, son!
I have wept a thousand times—
So much that no tears left are in my eyes.

Nine months passed,
The pain has amassed,
And the question in my heart lingers.

Hopeful? I tried.
I owe you my life.
Though I await your arrival,
I may not live to hold you in my hands.
I long for your cry when the sun falls back,
When the morning comes to rock you in my arms,
And when the silence calls to kiss you back to slumber.

How do I make up for wasted time?
For the wrong questions I asked?
The eerie feeling that I'm soon to be gone will not subside.

O', Jotham!
My Love, my life.
Your mother is radiant,
For your arrival is nigh.
In her cries, joy she will find,
For you shall be there to dry them away.

Fallen

Am I to be called a coward if I walk away?
Heart in throat,
Hyperthermia,
Blood in the head.
Pandemonium is the word,
Dreams buried by the beach palm.

If I wasn't warned,
The sun would never shine
And the moon would swallow the stars.
You have become my daylight
And my compass in the desert.

It's so gloomy in my head.
"If only I knew the truth," I thought,
"I would keep the light
And live my dreams."

Love

Love is faith
That dreams will come true.
You have to believe to hope for love.
Love is a precious gift
To cherish and treasure.
So hold on to love when you find yours.
Love is wonderful,
Like the candlelight, only shines
brighter when shared.
Love is beautiful,
Like the horizon in the countryside.
Love is heaven,
Like the air around us, it is everywhere.
Love is you,
And God is Love.

Alom

Almighty Alom:
Depth of the unknown,
Maze of eternal perspective,
Trumpet and sickle-selecting,
Hope of our beliefs.

O, Creator:
Holiest of holies,
Heavenly inhabitor,
Lord of host praises,
Daemon of my days.

All magnificence:
Meritorious munificence,
Sound of the seventh heavens,
Storm of the sixth caverns,
Muse of my creativity.

Supreme reality,
Kind of third diversity,
Mystique antique,
Cloud of thick mist,
Divinely inspiring.

Dynasty of peace,
Ancient sagacity uncease,
Booming thunder utterances,
White stallion rider,
Spirit of my insight.

Chapter 17

SAN DIEGO, CA: July 2014
Farewell, Navy

My Purpose

*I have followed the narrow path,
Away from the wide road.
In the valley,
I will find my purpose.
I may not know what awaits me
At the end of the broad road,
But no man could have two destinies.*

*How would I know the truth,
When my right could be wrong
Or my wrong could be right?
The ripples of my sin
Crawled to the edge of my destiny,
And all I could feel were the cracks in time
That I must get past.*

*The joy of life,
That this man may find his purpose here on Earth.
Like manna from heaven,*

Fill my soul like living bread.
And like a balloon
So light, I want to swim into the sky.
With my eyes closed, I want to step into heaven's gate,
'Cause I know what could be in store.

Three Years Long

Three years long,
I had closed my ears to my song.
In deeper sadness,
I held my hands faceless.
Overboard I fell,
Promising I'd sink lifeless.

I count ten years behind,
And I had walked that far back, sometimes.
Like a picture
Painted in the middle of an ocean,
My thoughts seem boundless.
Like a paddle ball,
Searching for a place to fall,
I chased the vision in my head.
Like the moment between life and death,
When you accept the imminent,
I hope to not fall into an abyss of unfathomable depth.

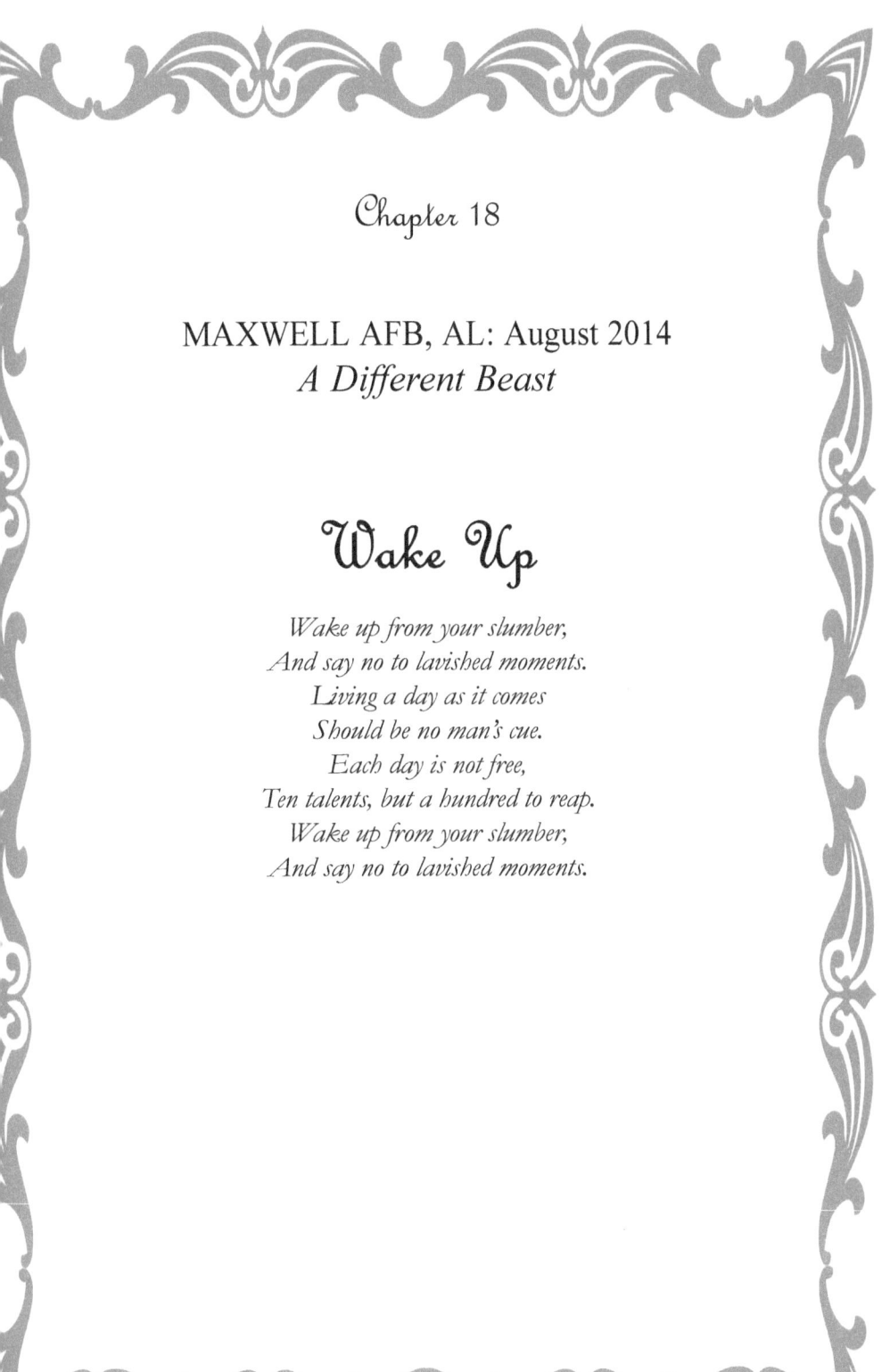

Chapter 18

MAXWELL AFB, AL: August 2014
A Different Beast

Wake Up

Wake up from your slumber,
And say no to lavished moments.
Living a day as it comes
Should be no man's cue.
Each day is not free,
Ten talents, but a hundred to reap.
Wake up from your slumber,
And say no to lavished moments.

The Love That I Found

How long has it been?
Up above the clouds,
His eyes have been.
I see the heavens from where I sit,
Wondering how I could watch still.

For every channel branching out from a river source,
I have no clue where the origin is.
Though my eagle glides faster than any car can go
And my crawl seems faster than my walk.

As I perceive the ugliness of the rocky expanse beneath me,
"She spreads to a world that she knew nowhere," I think to myself.
I imagine my daughter, my son, and my wife who gave them to me.
She will miss me still...
My children will remember me when they return home,
Because that's what kids do when they're finally away from other little ones.

My once deserted life that felt so empty,
Devoid of the kind of Love I desperately sought,
Now filled with the kind of life I only dreamt of as a child.
No matter what becomes of me from here on,
I know there will always be three of them that will never stop loving me,
So dearly, so unconditionally.

Chapter 19

MAXWELL AFB, AL: September 2014
The Sergeant Who Yelled

Déjà Vu

This world seems familiar,
Like I lived this life before now.
I've been here before, my heart tells me—
Maybe that's why I know where I want to be and where I don't.
I try to run far from what I thought I once knew—
Things that I dread and things I don't.
Even so, I try to run closer to my dreams;
I think they are a better path to my redemption,
The condition for which I have been given another life.
There's someone somewhere that I owe my existence,
For many tried to destroy but can't.

Beautiful Confliction

As I march through the windy marine
Way in the middle of the desert,
I see many faces made by the gentle washing of the rain.
It makes you wonder: where did they all go?
All I see are broken tracks and contours
Of what's left of the rock and clay:
Red, brown, and green.
Life couldn't be more complicated than the world below me,
But that's what makes it all beautiful.

PART 4:

Nuclear Missiles Operator

Chapter 20

VANDENBERG AFB, CA: October 2014
A "Doc" in Nuke "Tech" School

To whom is will safer?
Definitely not with us!
To whom much is given,
So little they have given back.

Music never dies,
As long as they are played.
Songs only have meanings
When they are written in words.

What gift could be greater?
To choose between good or bad,
Humanity or barbarism,
Morals or sin,
God or devil,
Love or hate,
To forgive or avenge,
To hope or to despair?

I Believe

I believe in the originality of man,
The vision of a far desert covering the sky,
The mystery of where the source of the ocean might be.
I can spend the rest of my life trying to understand nature.

I believe in preference,
Not by choice,
But by a force that could never be explained;
To choose to open a door
Rather than the other in a silent room.

I believe in the spirit,
And things it could probably wish for after death.
I believe in the discontentment of man,
'Cause, that's why we are so damn good at our gifts.
I believe in moderation,
'Cause the greatest sorrow comes from
Things we desire the most.

I believe in things we cannot change,
Even when we're closest to the edge of the sky.
The need to understand—
There is a greater force we will never comprehend!
My life can't explain itself,
But I have my dreams to hold on to.

There will never be such a thing as
"The greatest writer of all time."
Like we are not the same,
Words don't come out the same.

I don't believe in body language readers,
It's like trying to understand the heart
And the mind of all men at the same time.
Still, a gift is a gift.

There's no such thing as perfect Love,
But you can live your life for Love.
Children will continue to be innocent,
And more than always,
Will grow up to make good or bad examples.

I believe in technology;
It's changing the world.
Merely the users,
Seem like mini-gods.

I believe in traveling the world,
What could be a better way to express
The freedom of our mind,
And see with your eyes
How much of nature is at our disposal?

Chapter 21

VANDENBERG AFB, CA: January 2015
The Validator with an Accent

Forty Miles

I'm not scared of the world,
But I'm fearful of time
And what its ticking hands might do to me
Before I can seize it.

Ever felt like you're ending your future,
Where it should have started?
Have you ever looked back into your past
And wondered how on earth,
You missed so much?

Only if a man knew what he was meant to be,
Only if he knew who he is,
Only if circumstances yield to his heart,
Then he would dine and dance with fate.

More often than not, though,
Many oscillate forty long years—
To reach a forty-mile path?
Whatever special forces you believe in,
Whatever your faith is in,
May it order your steps.

Chapter 22

VANDENBERG AFB, CA: June 2015
The Veterinary Surgeon Became a Nuke Officer

The Man in the Mirror

Many moons have swept by,
Plus that dreary day we said goodbye.
And to think of the bye we bayed,
Those innocent eyes that caught my sight—
That calm, disciplined look that anchors tight.
That parting was very much a lousy bye.

Your magic makes me wonder about
Your charms and charisma.
And with this, I ponder
As my rain of euphoria falls so calm.
How can you be so lovingly cruel
To keep my heart all these years?
And hell, you made my sleep…

How much have I forgotten to love you?
For thousands of affections, I have bought you.
Now my restlessness is but yonder.
How foolish to act younger
When I should have shown my hunger,
Giving you my drive's power.

I could only write on paper,
But I'm a fumbler.
How to ever imagine this affection
That sticks without diversion?
You made me worth a prince.
A royalty given is not worth it,
Like pearls to the pigs.
And like a toddler in tantrums,
I furthered my malfunction.

But why myself do I condemn?
Heaven knows you are a thunder
That makes me blunder
As your sight causes uproar.
The mirror before me harbors the man,
Whose stand keeps me in a trance.
That's why I run around…

Then this night, you passed by,
And my sleeping head you made whirl.
This beautiful nightmare…
It gave me no time to keep there
That old cowardice.
I braved all when
I called you to show me a man who cares.
Yeah—those eyes tame still.
And yes, as a perfect man, I killed fear.

Wherever you are, you are still dear.
So much I yearn, but time's cord is lengthy yet.
Or is it that prayer locks you in here?
Remain, then—feel my soothing breath.
My soul is missing you.
My heart cries for you.

My body agonizes over your long absence.
My whole wish: Come home to me.
Come home. Man in the mirror. I'm waiting.

Chapter 23

F.E. WARREN AFB, WY: October 2015
The Deputy and His Commander

Snowstorm in May

Cheyenne is like a poem
Begging to be read.
She forces you under the blanket
With a paper and pen
As you try to comprehend the heart of the Midwest.

In the middle of May
Before the shoveling begins in the driveway,
You watch the snowflakes
As they fall on and around the new babes
Riding in the toboggan for the first time in the incline way.

Staring outside your window,
You wonder how beautiful the tree branches caught the snow,
And it's hard to put into words what the white earth holds.
It is a lovely thing to behold
When white Cheyenne in May glows.

Every Night without Light

For three nights,
It's been a full moon.
For three days,
It's been so cold.
And in all these moments,
It's been so gloomy.

The thoughts of the silence in my life,
Every night without light,
And my past in my mind,
All begging to be unleashed
By the unburdened quill in my tote
That burns in my heart.
It is time.

Chapter 24

F.E. WARREN AFB, WY: January 2017
The Nuke Officer and the Intercontinental Ballistic Missile (ICBM)

Joy of Utopia

By the macadam beaching the bay,
She walks nimbly and weakly today.
Though I say today, nay! but allay.
Dreaming a dummy, wake to reality.
Crossing the bumpy?
Where's fidelity?
O, joy of Utopia.

If only we could have
No death and no rivalry,
No sadism and no racism,
No prejudice and no ethnocentrism,
No renegism and no prodigality—
All on deuce, none on nil.
O, joy of Utopia.

Would I see her? Would I hear her?
Rejoicing with much hilarity,

My absurd nation of penuriousness.
Who will make her one?
Where is the don?
Will we ever find one—
one to create our Utopia?

Nine Years Ago

Nine years ago, you left forever.
But then, I followed your last words.
I left too but in a very different way,
for a path you deeply desired for me
That I would only wish for myself nonetheless.

I finally dared to stare deep into your eyes
As I held your pictures.
I searched for a picture of us together,
But I couldn't find any.
However, I wish I could.
A lesson learned now that I am a dad…
It doesn't matter anymore, though,
'Cause you're always in my heart, dad.
I miss you.

Epilogue

WASHINGTON, D.C.: October 2018
The Father I Became

I heard of the river on the mountain:
Pellucid and still, shallow, and warm.
Take me there and lay me rest...

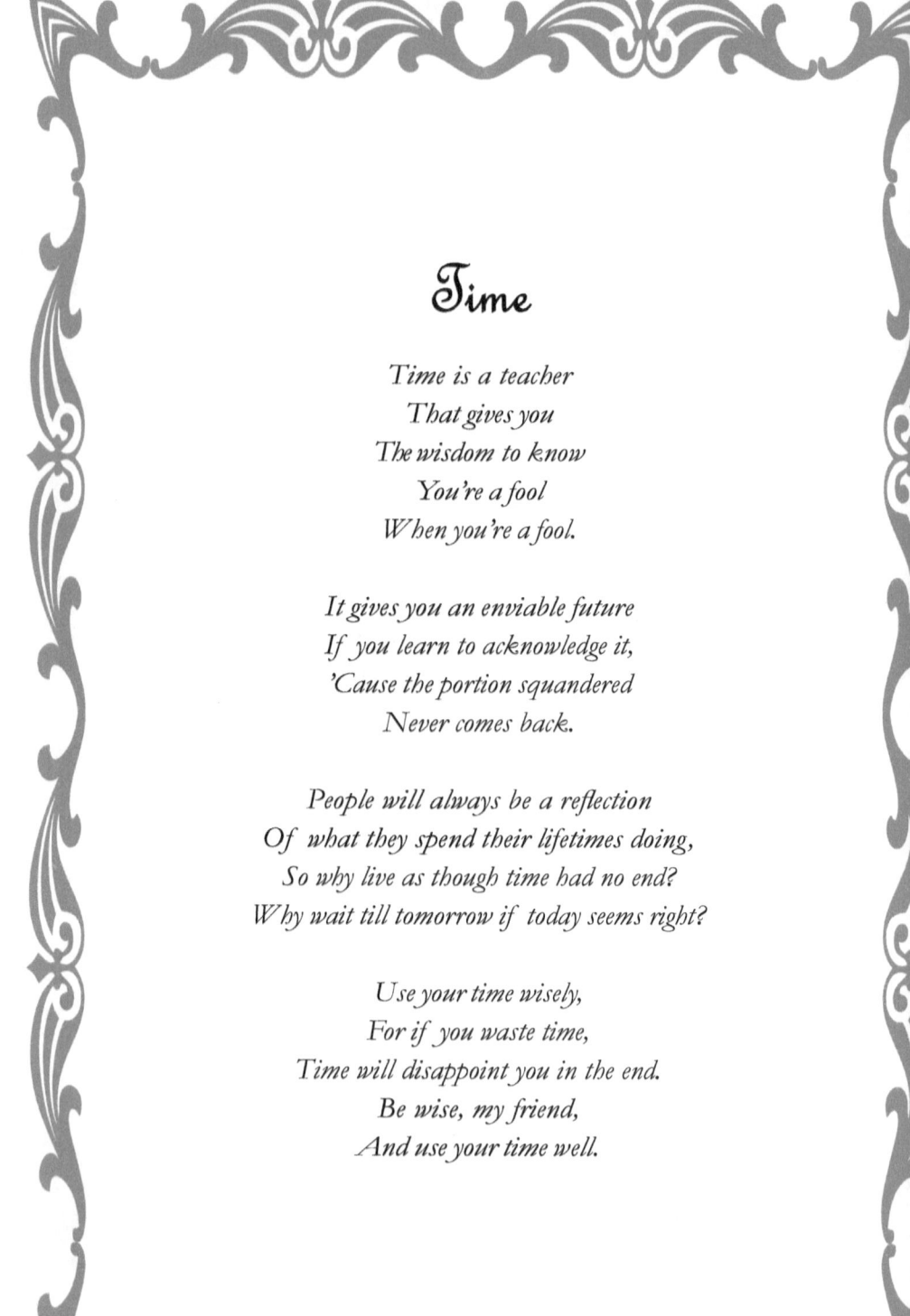

Time

Time is a teacher
That gives you
The wisdom to know
You're a fool
When you're a fool.

It gives you an enviable future
If you learn to acknowledge it,
'Cause the portion squandered
Never comes back.

People will always be a reflection
Of what they spend their lifetimes doing,
So why live as though time had no end?
Why wait till tomorrow if today seems right?

Use your time wisely,
For if you waste time,
Time will disappoint you in the end.
Be wise, my friend,
And use your time well.

Past Heroes

I can hear them;
I can see them.
Like a sound from a broken pipe
Came the cries from dust.
Like rain
Came the tears from the sky.
The broken-hearted widow to be
And the unfulfilled promises!

Father!
That's what you are.
Love!
Yes! So intense you sacrificed all.
And Liberty!
The reason for it all.
A foundation for a new generation,
The best gift to any child.

The flesh might turn ashes,
And the bones might return to dust,
But the spirit will always endure.
The glory will live on,
So that the glorious can be engraved in gold.
I'd choose an immortal name
Over all the treasures of the world.

Lost

Help me—
I'm traveling a one-way road.
Though lost on my trail,
I want to keep moving on.
My limbs get weaker,
So I keep crawling on my knees.
My shredded skin has bled,
Staining the sand red,
Yet it will take a miracle to see you.

Since your time has come,
Then mine's a forlorn hope.
The loss is mine,
And that's because we had
Only twenty days between us.

The Lagos-Island Beauty

I can hear the cockcrow and see
Streams of gold running past the blinds.
It's time for my friends to fly out of their nests.
The Beautiful City of Lagos,
Friends, and roses,
But you seem to be my first thought.
Grandma, Grandma,
The Island Beauty.

It's more beautiful in the woods
When autumn leaves.
Red flowers?
It's anthocyanin!
Christmas illusions?
Grandma, Grandma,
Your beauty stretches farther than the eye can see.

Grandma,
Did I mention how old you are now?
I want you to know:
My heart reaches out to you always.
Though I'm so far away,
It will always be with you.
I'll never leave you to frailty,
My Island Beauty.

Dear Dad

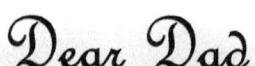

Dearly beloved father,
It's been eight years today
Since you've been gone.
I held your flowers by your grave,
Your words still engraved in my heart.

Like it happened only yesterday,
I stared at the smile traces
Left on your departed face.
You left my arms, My hands,
And I am standing six feet
From the edge of your new home.

I can't imagine how lonely
You have been for eight years.
Eight years I have missed you,
Eight years more I have lived,
'Cause you're gone!

Four Seasons in a Day

The sun reflects on the melting snow.
The leafless trees bend to the whistle of the wind.
And what becomes of the creases on the tarred roads
Is not much of a worry meant for them.
However, the wheels that run over them
While enduring four seasons in one day is.

Selah!

Every time I close my eyes,
I want to live a perfect moment of my life.

You took a nail in the sky,
Where my losses died.
You gave me peace,
But my soul couldn't see.
You gave me shelter;
Your Love, where you wanted me forever.
You called me your child,
But like a bastard,
I never obliged.
You raised me a family
And proved you love me truly.

Still, you fill my soul with gladness
I'd never find anywhere else.

Selah! Selah!
I hear your voice calling.
Selah! Selah!
And in my heart, singing.
All you ask of me
Is a moment to pause and think.

About the Author

Dr. 'Deji Ayoade is an emerging memoir author and lifelong poet who strives to touch the lives of his readers through heartfelt poetic storytelling. In addition to his memoir and companion poetry book, he is the author of *Selah! Selah! (Pause and Think): Poetry*.

Enduring a childhood chock-full of impoverishment and loss, poetry was his safe haven, quickly becoming his way of envisioning a future he wanted to be a part of. Moreover, the power of the written word served as reassurance that he and his loved ones would one day leave all the hardship in Nigeria behind.

Writer aside, 'Deji Ayoade has held the roles of Veterinary Surgeon, Combat Medic, Nuclear Weapon System SME, Senior Program Analyst, and U.S. Space Force Department of Defense Civilian.

Poems from Underground is an emotive journey of restored hope and faith along the path of attaining the American Dream and communion with a higher power that was there all along. Page by page, a personal narrative is revealed to the reader—one brimming with trials and triumphs, grief and joy, loss and love in equal measure. Through poignant, candid, and vulnerable storytelling, 'Deji Ayoade shares his innermost stirrings of the heart and all the maelstroms they entail with utmost poise. Beyond a mere poetry collection of outpourings by an American military man, this is a true story about a soul who, since birth, envisioned a thriving future for himself and the generations to come.